The Jane and Bertha in Me

The Jane and Bertha in Me

Poems by

Rita Maria Martinez

Kelsay Books

Cover Art: "Two Sides of the Same Coin" by Kate O'Keefe
Visit her website: http://kate-okeefe.weebly.com

ISBN 13:978-0692543412

Kelsay Books
Aldrich Press
www.kelsaybooks.com

to Brontëites who love Jane

for Jose and Mery, my parents, who support my writing

for Todd, my husband and a librarian who has longed

to catalogue this book

Acknowledgments

I would like to thank the editors and staff members of the publications in which these poems, some with slightly different titles, first appeared:

Kaleidoscope, **Issue #72:** "The Literature of Prescription" 2016
Gravel: "Alice Fairfax in Wonderland" 2015
2River View, **Issue 19.5:** "Jane's Denial" and "Jane
    Responds When Asked, *Why Edward?*" 2015
The Hamilton Stone Review, **Issue 33:** "Governess-to-Go,"
    "Catching Edward," "Jane Eyre in the Jungle Room," "Letter
    to Edward," and *"I Am Thine, Charles Thunder"* 2015
ndREview (Online Companion to the Notre Dame Review for
    Issue 40*):* "Jane Eyre Thinks of Tarzan's Jane" and "Marsh
    End Priestess" 2015
Doctor T.J. Eckleburg Review: "Jane Dreams of Laci Peterson"
    2015
Apalachee Review, **65:** "Jane Eyre: Classic Cover Girl" 2015
Gargoyle, **#64:** "The Madwoman" 2015
Cantologia 1, Amor: "Jane Dreams of Rescuing Helen." An
    anthology published by Pandora Lobo Estepario Productions
    featuring authors who have participated in the *Palabra
    Pura* reading series sponsored by the Guild Literary Complex in
    Chicago, 2013
MiPOesias, American Cubans: "Blanche Ingram's Bitterness"
    and "Postmortem Lament for Charlotte" 2011
MiPOesias: "Fashion Remedy," "St. John Rivers Pops the
    Question," and "Reading *Jane Eyre* II" 2008
MiPOesias, All Ladies Issue, **Vol. 20, Issue 2:** *"Principes Negros
    de Juana"* 2006
MiPOesias, MiPO Print Companion, **Vol. 19, Issue 1:** "Letter to
    Bertha," "Cause and Effect," "Nautica," and "Reading *Jane
    Eyre*" 2005
Mangrove, **No. 13:** "Jane Addresses Edward" 2004
Diagram, **3.2:** "Vintage Bertha Triptych" and "Mortification
    Triptych" 2003

Some of the poems in *The Jane and Bertha in Me* were also published by the late Richard Bixby of March Street Press in 2008 as a chapbook titled *Jane-in-the-Box*.

The poem "St. John Rivers Pops the Question" was nominated for a Pushcart Prize in 2008.

The poem "Reading *Jane Eyre* II" received an honorable mention in AWP's *Writer's Chronicle* for the 2002 Intro Journals Project.

I am also grateful to the following individuals for their criticism, enthusiasm, and kindness: Campbell McGrath, Denise Duhamel, the faculty at Florida International University, Marilyn Hoder-Salmon, Jeannine Hall Gailey, Marcia Southwick, Kristina Martinez, Francisco Aragón, Emma Trelles, Abigail Martin, Richard Ryal, Jay Snodgrass, Mary Ann Baker, Hugo Rodriguez, Wayne Loshusan, Debra Woolley, Alexandra Lytton, Roy Guzmán, Caridad Moro, Mia Leonin, Norman Minnick, Nin Andrews, Gonzalo Barr, Lissette Mendez, and Jen Karetnick.

Contents

Promiscuous Reading

I could not help it; the restlessness was in my nature. Then my sole relief was to walk along the corridor of the third story, backwards and forwards, safe in the silence and solitude of the spot, and allow my mind's eye to dwell on whatever bright visions rose before it—and, certainly, they were many and glowing; to let my heart be heaved by the exultant movement, which, while it swelled it in trouble, expanded it with life; and, best of all, to open my inward ear to a tale that was never ended—a tale my imagination created, and narrated continuously . . . .

—from *Jane Eyre*, Charlotte Brontë

Femme Covert

Reading *Jane Eyre*

I covered it with clear contact paper,
wrote my name in caps across the foredge in black marker.
The bloated book rested on my desk like a rainbow trout.
Mrs. Lloyd poised on the stool, her bangs and bob stiff
like a man in a toupee, face primed with a thick coat
of concealer. She hinted a secret at the heart of the text—
I spotted it in her eyes whenever she laughed,
flung her arms like tentacles, crossed her legs,
private insanity hidden inside her wisteria wool
skirt, tucked out of sight like Thornfield's third-floor
tenant, Linda Blair's precursor, the basket case languishing in bed.
I read in bed, on the bamboo love seat, beneath the shade
of my father's banana trees. I scarfed the pages like pork rinds,
yuca chips, crackers slathered with guava jelly.
I binged constantly, sunk my canines into text
while Blur's *Boys and Girls* wailed in the background like Bertha
on speed. I carried it for weeks inside the outer pocket
of my Eastpack like Tic Tacs, a compact I'd flip open
during lunch, between classes, before soccer practice—Bantam
paperback lodged between *Agnes Grey* and *Wuthering Heights*
at Adolph's bookstore, its spine red-orange like papaya pulp.
I plucked it from the shelf and stared at the cover—
the forlorn wedding dress yearning for Jane's scapula,
her small breasts, the warmth of her hips when she walks
across the bedroom and steps into wedding slippers,
then into absence, the foot's descent consuming as quicksand,
the subtle curve of her arch sheathed by glass.

The Jane and Bertha in Me

The Jane in me wants to model a black dress,
bottle-thick lenses, tuck my hair in a bun.

The Bertha in me wants to sport a turban,
a red nightgown, and chandelier earrings.

The Jane in me is suspicious of men flaunting
pinkie rings, each diamond the size of a Chiclet.

The Bertha in me believes leathery hands barnacled
with gypsy rings are an omen of fertility.

The Jane in me seizes meaning in the curve
of a nose, the stain of a birthmark on the scalp,

interprets the stitch of hair standing to attention
on the back of a stranger's head, reads bushy eyebrows,

the wide mouth to mean he is stubborn,
eats salad with his hands and continues speaking

regardless of tomato basil soup dribbling
down his chin. The Bertha in me sleeps

until three in the afternoon and sits on the back porch
with a cup of Earl Grey that quells the desire to chop

up her crotchety landlord. The Bertha in me contemplates
the moon, constellations perched on the cusp of night

like hundreds of stretched hands on an assembly
line, like synchronized swimmers suspended in mid-stroke,

while the Jane in me wants to extract Rochester's teeth
with her Tweezerman, stow them in a jar,

a pillbox, deposit his wrenched incisors
and canines in a velvet pouch and pin it to her bra

so she can feel his presence, so she can lay
that satchel on her pillow and wake each morning

to the prayer of his teeth marks on her pale cheek.

The Guidance Counselor Interrogates Jane

She of the nervous tick, the Larry King
look-alike with pleated pants hiked to the neck
sits at her desk, arms folded, staring disinterestedly
at your file the same way the bored do at tabloids
under the oppressive lights of Walmart,
their glazed eyes landing on the latest Elvis sighting.
A senior at a small private school, this is the first time
you're summoned to her lair. Though accomplished,
you're not a stellar superstar, not valedictorian
material, nor in the top five. A blip on this crone's radar,
circumstance delivers you to the obligatory meeting.
When she inquires about your intended major,
English slips from your lips, countered by the dreaded
What are you going to do with that, teach?
which floats in the air like a bad case of mono waiting for a host.
Not sure, you say, crossing your legs, fearing brainwashing,
transfixed by the disturbing folds of her neck which conjure
even more disturbing images of the Scientology chicken
featured on *Late Night with Conan O'Brien.*
This is when the words *technical writer* slip from her lips,
though you doubt she'd advise her Brat Pack
to crank out instructions for operating CD players
or assembling IKEA furniture. You can't imagine writing
about kitchen appliances from 9 to 5, delineating the nuance
between mix and purée for masses of Paula Dean proselytes,
or being riveted by the nuts and bolts of a life without literature,
one where each peg is inserted into its predetermined slot.

Fashion Remedy

Jane's grown weary of lingeried mannequins,
of women spritzing her like exterminators,

of Burdines, Macy's, Saks blazing before her.
Sweat pools beneath each plum-sized

breast as she crosses a continent of asphalt
to reach the rented Honda, its treacherous

seat belt that digs into her shoulder like a cheap bra.
She sits in silence waiting for the traffic light's

transformation from heat wave to go-go
when Eddie's crumpled, razor-burned face

appears in the rear view mirror, his scarred forehead
hot as the steering wheel against her fingertips.

She parts her lips, ready to stitch soothing syllables
across the steaming cicatrix, sew secrets

into his skin, a grocery list of things she wishes
to forget: the gold-digger got suckered

into a sour deal, landed a Loch Ness monster,
a loony Jezebel, a homicidal hoochie, hysterical

juju woman, schitzo, succubus, suicidal skank
to have and to hold, to love and to honor,

to cherish and obey *la sucia* hidden like the mole
on his inner thigh, mothballs beneath the bed,

the leftover plate of lasagna forgotten in the freezer.
If she takes him back he'll beg for forgiveness,

he'll say he loves her, he'll take liberties,
call her *Janet* or *Janey* though she hates it.

He'll shower her with garter belts
from Victoria's Secret as if sprinkling

croutons across salad, he'll decorate her like a Christmas tree,
insist she wear the silver arm cuff, those topaz earrings

that dangle from her lobes like fishing
lures. When he gets bored he'll scrunch her

like a candy bar wrapper, toss her in his fishbowl.
It's good I'm safe, she thinks, as she removes

her lips from the mirror, grabs a bottle of Evian
from the car's cup holder and chugs.

It's good you're in there, and I'm out here, she tells Eddie
as she licks her lips and the light blinks green.

Jane Dreams of Laci Peterson

Captivated by stories of abusive relationships,
of mysterious deaths and missing persons,
I watched late night programs like *Wicked Attraction,*
The New Detectives, and *Deadly Women.*
Fascinated by blood splatter theory, gunpowder residue,
fingerprint bruises on abandoned female corpses,
I hoped to crack the code behind Bertha's unabashed cackle,
wondered if I could cope with Eddie's cockamamie
plan to keep her a caged gerbil. One evening I caught
a recap on Laci's fate: the bay slowly erasing her features
as her husband nonchalantly purchased and watched
snuff films, streamed an endless parade of women
on his high def screen, their faces eventually blurring
like Laci's. He could barely remember what the wife
looked like—though her photo was plastered everywhere,
so pretty and pregnant in that little black cocktail dress.
Finally, the decomposed body surfaced,
limbs drifting like disembodied mannequin parts.
After the baby washed ashore, those at the morgue admired
its perfectly formed fingernails, its golden eyelashes
which flooded my thoughts, then my dreams, for months.
Always the same image: Conner's eyelashes dissolving
into a warm, golden light enveloping Laci,
who eternally sleeps on a bed of sand, seashells
nestled and glowing in her hair.

Thinking of Bertha on the Metro

—The prisoner in solitary confinement—the toad in the
block of marble—all in time shape themselves to their lot.
(Charlotte Brontë to W.S. Williams; letter dated July 26, 1849)

A woman reads the obits,
another *¡Hola!* magazine, and the lady
with beautiful braids announces
Listen up people on this train:
Jesus loves you, yes, He does!
as passengers board on and off.
Nauseated amidst the grandmother smell
of the woman beside me, I think of you
in the psych ward, wilted and tangled
in the bed's odorless sheet and blanket.
Funny how some of us hang
on by the skin of our teeth. I open my plastic
pill box and swallow a white oval,
the ones that seem to jump from my hand
on mornings when I'm in a hurry.
At night I crawl on all fours,
fish for those bits of fleeting peace
as I would a missing earring.
I think of your brother placing a green
Saint Jude scapular around your neck,
how you will wake in the middle
of the night, that square of plastic pinching
your skin because you sleep face down,
head buried beneath the pillow,
though you plot escape as we all do,
as I do when I bury myself in a book
or glance past the train's filthy window
wondering what I've missed.

Jane Eyre in the Jungle Room

Jane floats about like a young
Priscilla at Graceland, lives
His lifestyle though her ring finger

is barren and the driveway
doesn't boast a Mercedes Roadster,
nor a pink go-cart. She refuses

to pile on the Cleopatra liner
capped with six layers of lashes.
Clarity is elusive, so she leaves

the falsies to Blanche's bickering
entourage. The King wants her
here, but Jane wants to disappear

amidst the menagerie of monkeys
whose yellowish eyes capture all;
longs to evaporate, pull a Houdini

among these ghostly mascots
purchased by E's ex-girlfriend,
the same nut-job who doled

cold cash for the lurid Tiki loveseat,
the couch with dragon arms,
green shag on the floor and ceiling

resembling moss. Jane prays for
deliverance from coffee and chatter
when the raven-haired ring leader

and her high-class hags slander her
as if she were invisible—a light mist
barely occluding their vision. Best to fly

under the radar, comply in the corner,
head down, knitting needles in hand
before the Big E baits beautiful Blanche.

Cross-Dressing

Perhaps Freud thought the pen was a penis
in the hand of pseudonymous writers like Currer Bell—
perhaps Miss Brontë was merely a cross-dresser,
the transvestite equivalent of Rochester in gypsy drag:
his hoop earrings and rose quartz bracelets jingling
as he hypnotizes Jane by brandishing a fire opal amulet.

Did Currer Bell have penis envy?
Maybe she envied efficiency,
men quickly tucking their penises in their trousers,
dispensing with fiddling through multiple layers
of clothing. Men and women, authors of their own fiction,
envisioned Currer Bell a cross between Rochester and Rivers—
imagined both men recipients of a bizarre organ donation—
Bell's body parts scattered between a polygamist
and a missionary, the buzz reaching C.B., the victim
of a recurrent nightmare:

Currer Bell stands in a large crowd
wearing a stick-on mustache and a bathrobe.
His girdle gives, slithers down the slope of his legs
to rest in a crumpled heap, feet encircled by waves
of pink satin that surge against his hamstrings and quads
whenever he bends over to pick up his favorite pen
(the one with his initials engraved, a gift from a secret admirer).
The baby blue flower on that girdle winks at Currer
with the same expression that flickers across Bertha's face
as she's perched on Thornfield's roof like it's Mount Olympus,
surveying the thickness of neighboring clouds,

then diving into the unknown. Bell laments the unhappy
marriage—the elastic digging into his small waist
like Blanche Ingram's French-manicured nails—
and, for the life of him, he can't decide whether he wants to slip
into that girdle like he's sliding into home,
or kick it under the sofa while everyone's on all fours
distracted, combing the carpet for his missing pen.

Rochester Triptych

1. Oh My Little Girl

At first it was curiosity, whim.
I wanted to know if she was a private
school girl with public school pizzazz,
fire and ice, you know the kind:
ankle-length skirts, panties optional.

Tenacious of life, eager plums,
these Lowood girls.

It was never a question of looks.
Not much to tempt a man—
except perhaps the curve of her neck,
vanilla pudding skin, pale and soft
as Millcote's silk for sale.

She was no Céline Varens.
She was no Blanche Ingram.

2. Jane-in-the-Box

A sequestered pet, rabbity
once liberty is granted.
Flexible as a Slinky,
cottony voice
the sound of knives
severing fresh bread.
She loved silly popsicles,
the smear of rainbowed
lips and tongue.

Her pearl choker limp as a dead eel.
She pitied each strand, each pearl
plucked from its ivory bed,
beads for ditzy wind-up dolls.
Girls like Céline, Giacinta or Clara—
Comtesse, Signorina, Gräfina—
perfumed, powdered, pumiced.

She is V-necks, fishnets, lace-up
boots coating her calves like cake frosting.
After standing by the maple chestnut door
like an expectant dog, she stuffed
pillows beneath the eiderdown,
opened the window, slipped between the bars
like a thin slice of toast.

3. Fairy Tattoo

When I find the fugitive nymph
I will bracelet her wrists,
garnish her fingers with marquisette,
brand my initials across her wings.
Though words will tumble
from her tongue, her brandied voice
will pour over me. She is wild thyme,
a bonfire, puffs of air spiraling
through the flute's reed.
Yesterday, I thought I spotted her
in a blooming rosebush.

Jane Addresses Edward

—I could not, in those days, see God for his creature of whom I'd made an idol.
(from *Jane Eyre*, Charlotte Brontë)

What you don't know is that I tossed
my wedding veil from the window,
witnessed its inevitable descent,
speck of tulle splayed against
ground like a wounded wren.

What you don't know is that
I pecked morsels like a pigeon;
a strapless bra slid off my deflated chest,
my nipples were sharp crayon tips scribbling
farewells across an untucked blouse.

What you don't know is that I missed
the meticulous chop and shred
of late suppers, the smile that flared
when thoughts of snapping me
in half like a wishbone flitted in your head.

What you don't know is that I stalked
stores, scoured shelves for the appropriate
shawl, a partner to sympathize with:
fabric frayed as your first wife.

The sky was a tipped cauldron
weeping over silent moors.
Head down, chin tucked, careful not
to glance back lest I turn to salt,
I waded through mud, clawed
rotting wood of mute thresholds.

Outside the local bakery I leaned my palms
against the wet windowpane like suction
cups and stared at the sweet display:
gingermen reposing on white strips of parchment—
insubstantial specimens, miniature
sugared corpses coming to life.

Nautica

I was walking toward the post
when a guy whizzed by like a messenger.
I can't tell you what he looked like
or what he wore, only that the scent
of his cologne lingered as if saying *hello*—
and that he smelled like you, like the blue flask
of Nautica you kept in the glove
compartment, like my purple turtleneck
on nights I sank into bed carrying
your scent the way little girls
carry dolls to their beds, the way men
carry loose change in their pockets
all day, without realizing.

Mortification Triptych

1. Master John Reed Punishes Jane for Hiding in the
   Curtained Window Seat and Reading His Copy of Bewick's
   History of British Birds

She's nestled by the window. She's light as a celery stick. Nothing
between them but this scarlet shroud. She wants to wedge her flesh
between the folds when he parts the curtains and snatches the
volume. Its *shores of Lapland, Siberia, Spitzbergen, Nova Zembla,
Iceland* dangle in midair, morph into a meat cleaver. She flies
toward the locked door. Poised in his grubby hand, the picture
book becomes a hacksaw—its teeth glittering like JR's eyes when
he decapitates doves in the yard. His dragon breath hovers.
Bewick's *History* soars across the breakfast room, a Chinese star
slicing her scalp. Fire spews from his nostrils. She's splayed across
the carpet, *a bird rending its own plumage*. On the back of her
neck, blood sizzles; she smears it beneath her eyes like war paint.
She flaps her wings in the dragon's face and claws her initials
across his arm. Her beak gleams through smoke. The breakfast
room splattered with feathers, scales and ash.

2. Locked in the Red Room

She crawls beneath the garnet couch, hides like an abandoned rag
doll, the missing clasp on her favorite dress, a base coat of nail
polish, a clitoris, lice latched onto a stranger's hair, a solitary sock,
the nipple capped by a child's mouth, a penny, her uncle's letters
ripening in a drawer like wild berries, the mattress cowering
beneath its Marseilles comforter, termites crunching the mahogany
vanity, sinking their teeth into chairs carved for the benefactress,
sawing through the rash between her toes as she rubs her feet
across the crimson carpet again and again trying to smother an

invisible fire, stamp out spirits seeping through the barred windows, the brick chimney, the bolted door, dead relatives draining the spark of her thoughts—their fleeting brilliance diving off the lip of this crater, this exile among rosewood jewel caskets, blushing walls, and sanguine shadows.

3. Sentenced to the Stool

Treacherous slate, cold slab for math sandpapers her chilblains, slips through her fingers, becomes a soft-bodied lamprey glissading before Brocklehurst's feet, the Holy Moly instructing everyone to blacklist her, treat her like a Jane Doe, but she's so nervous and pitiful, she pees until her skirt is a wet wash cloth, fears he'll slap her forehead as if banging a jammed cash register, make her kneel on a bed of rice—instead he orders her to the stool where her totem pole body wilts as droopy Lowood girls sitting at desks upchuck shillings, deposit them up the math tutor's nostrils until she expectorates soda cans for everyone but Jane, who's still on the stool, watching equations writhing on chameleon chalkboards that stampede out the room, while cold air sweeps through the open windows tempting her to scratch an itchy scalp, her alert nipples, those tired ankles staring at the tarnished buckles of her Mary Janes, rows of MJs nailed to the ceiling, walls, floor, oh she fears those innocent shoes with slick foreheads, hollow necks, and gaping mouths will drown her in their parched throats.

Hitchhiking Across L.A.

First three buttons on her blouse undone.
Hip-huggers and chain belt coated with pixie dust.
She shoplifted Chanel's Infrarouge Whisperlight
because tonight she wants to glow.
He pulls up and flashes his lights.
Tortoiseshell headband poised as a tiara,
she holds her head like Grace Kelly,
wonders if she should've paid more attention
during *America's Most Wanted*. In her backpack
outer compartment: two bucks, granola bar,
can of mace. Moonlight flits off the patent leather
of her Mary Janes. Her fingers touch the door.
The road dissolves behind her as she is
swallowed by the creamy Camaro.

I Am Thine, Charles Thunder

is how Charlotte signs a letter for BFF Ellen Nussey.
Slipping into disguise is second nature for C.B. in 1836,
yet there's always a hint of truth surrounding
Brontë's mystery men. In Greek, her name means thunder.
Charles Thunder is a suave fast-talker.
Raven hair slicked, decked in requisite
Boss or impeccable Armani,
I imagine Mr. Thunder is actually Zeus playing
hooky among the roulette wheels and neon lights
of Vegas, a busty broad dangling from each bicep blowing
on his dice. Thunder the kind who thinks nothing
of leaning over, softly kissing a woman's hand
and whispering, *Your room or mine?*

Jane's Denial

*. . . [it] is truly humiliating, not to know how to get mastery
over one's own thoughts, to be the slave of a regret, a memory.*
(Charlotte Brontë to Constantin Héger; letter dated November 18, 1845)

Pain caused by first love never truly subsides.
Cunning and deceptive, it lurks dormant
until you've made peace with the alternate life
you could've led, fully loaded with hubby,
home, the 2.5 children *he* named (Isabel, Iris,
Inés) though you weren't even sure you wanted
kids then. Just when you've mastered
eating with chopsticks, are able to rise from bed,
have rediscovered flossing, are singing and humming
to the Beach Boys on the car radio—heck,
maybe you're wearing an engagement ring,
are buying *His* and *Hers* monogrammed towels,
just then, you run into the old bastard
and the unchristian desire to claw
his eyes returns natural as breathing.

The Gothic Grotesque

The Madwoman

—*Bertha is not my name. You are trying to make me into someone
else, calling me by another name.* (from *Wide Sargasso Sea,* Jean Rhys)

After Tenaya Darlington

Alcoholic adulteress, attic inmate, aberration, antagonistic
bitch, belligerent banshee, bewildered Bridezilla.
Clitoridectomy candidate confined to the coercion chair.
Daughter-in-law. Dildo addict. Darwinian example of devolution.
Emasculating exhibitionist. Earth's excrement. Eccentric with
   enlarged cerebellum.
Femme covert. Ferocious fiend foaming at the mouth.
Gangrened gash. Gibberish-spouting genius. Grotesque guinea pig.
Hypochondriac. Hysterical Hepzibah haunting the halls.
Irresponsible breeder. Irrational imbecile inebriated by *Eau de
   Cologne.*
Jane-in-the-box. Jinxed Jezebel. Junkie supermodel
Kate Moss. Klimt's contorted woman. Klingon chomping on
   men's bones.
Lesbian. Lactating liability. Lust-ridden lunatic listless from
   leaching of the labia.
Muzzled manic. Masturbator. Maudsley's menstruating Medusa.
Neurasthenic nada. Nut job. Nympho. Nun.
Ogre. Opium eater. Ovarian
prisoner. Poetess predestined to promiscuity, paranoid
queen of cuckooland convinced
ravens rip into her right arm when resting.
Secluded. Screw-gagged. Silenced by scold bridle.
Testosterone-driven tidal wave teetering toward
uterine dysfunction. Urchin identifiable by unsymmetrical
vulva. Volcanic, Valiumed, vivisected. Virgin veiling
warped wisdom. Wackadoos like Wollstonecraft, Woolf,
   Winehouse.
Xanaxed, Generation X girl
yammering away, your mind a rusty
zipper, byproduct of a defective zygote.

Vintage Bertha Triptych

1. Bertha Versus Mason

—She said she'd drain my heart.
    (from *Jane Eyre,* Charlotte Brontë)

The spiderback chair faces the fireplace.
    Flames unfurl like peacock feathers.
He rubs his arm on the spot where
    his sister's teeth marks are fossilized,
taps his fingers against the shot glass
    between sips of Jamaican rum.
The glare reminds him of her swollen
    eyes gleaming with warped moonlight.
Just before the chandelier crystals crashed
    like cymbals then drooped like wilted chrissies.
Just before she forked her nails into his chest
    as if stabbing a piece of mutton.

2. Bertha Torches Thornfield

—You can't be hidden away all your life.
    (from *Wide Sargasso Sea,* Jean Rhys)

Eyes closed, head bowed, arms
outstretched to channel the elements,
she sways like an empty hammock,
flickers like the transitory radiance
of daylight about to be snuffed.

She tosses the stolen candle
onto the battlement like a stick
of dynamite, leans over the precipice,
hair draping her face,

and whispers a brief prayer,
the only words capable of pulsing
past her parched lips: *Coulibri, bamboo,*
frangipanni, vetiver, sangoree.

Flames like Spanish Town sunsets,
tongues of fire cascading
from the roof like ripcords
can't save her, as she dives,
a crazed pterodactyl.

3. Ode to Bertha Antoinette Mason

Your mandarin voice resonates
among the *chinoiserie escritoire,*
the spiced meat stew, silver toothpicks,
spikes of spun sugar, bedizened scarecrows
and giggling fountains in shaggy gardens,
in the phosphorescent silence of mausoleums,
in their cavalcade of corpses: shepherd
boys, gypsy lads, chignoned priests,
lovely cartomancers with waxen fingers,
their whorled prints frozen on *La Papesse,*
La Morte, La Tour Abolie.
O moonless voracious huntress,
O moth-ravaged mistress,
men want to kiss the wormy oak of your harpsichord mouth
as mauvish evening sheds its submarine radiance.

41

Principes Negros de Juana

After your proposal, red quivering emissaries
swaddled in transparent cellophane arrive.
I descend the escalators cradling them
like Miss America. *Congrats!* chimes a stranger.
The garnet ambassadors rest on my lap
while I ride the Metro, foliage peeping,
fronds lightly brushing my elbows.
If I bend the wrong way the buds will bob
backwards, perhaps snap as I enter
the car. I drive like there's a baby
in back. Before undressing the roses,
before soaking fatigued stems,
I notice cylinders inserted at the base of each—
liquid capsules preventing your silent
envoys from premature wilting,
shielding them from this precarious life.

Blanche Ingram's Bitterness

Their engagement portrait and my modeling pics are smeared
across the tabloids like bird shit on a windshield.

That smug mug, Miss Hoytoytoy's blotchy pinched face
makes me puke. Never trust anyone named Jane—

especially a loose tooth who futzes with her fork
and doesn't know how to butter her bread.

Good riddance to him and his French freeloader,
says mom. *You're in the bloom of youth, honey bunny.*

Snag someone else. Someone younger. Richer.
With a six-pack. Without eczema.

Can't take a drag or wet my whistle without bumping
into the pair or getting the skinny on their squirrel

fever from club phonies. The love doves even planted their tails
in front of me at a funeral service. Miss Sloppy Seconds

nestled her head on his shoulders and gawked at her pitiful
engagement ring like it was the eighth wonder of the world.

I wouldn't shell out any dough for that paltry pebble.
Word is the grand Mister R is up to his ascot

in back taxes and hawked his Santa Cruz
stogies so he could rock her.

Alice Fairfax in Wonderland

After Franco Mondini-Ruiz's *Crystal City*

In the china cabinet, heirlooms
inherited by my master's mother and by her
mother before her. Following the dictates of duty,
I supervise the monthly polishing of silver.
Last week the master discovered a stray finger
print on the silver-plated serving tray.
I think the new girl is to blame.
Bits of filigreed finery infiltrate my dreams.
A butter knife rings the doorbell. A candy dish
sprouts eyes. A pair of skulls converse
on the cake pedestal. Sometimes
I wake at midnight, then rise and count
each piece of cool stemware that leans
toward my touch like a wistful tulip.
I always ascertain the tea service faces west.
Early evenings I verify the serving spoon doesn't grow
claws as I reach for it, suppertime so unpredictable here.

Cause and Effect

Because Bertha's left hip is higher
than the right, she measures the pool
water's pH every day. Because
her right breast is larger than the left,
she's skeptical of new and improved
laundry detergent, of buy-one-
get-one-free advertisements.
She puckers, she contours, she slathers
her kisser with Pink Panther lipstick
before slipping under plaid quilts
because there's a macaroni-shaped scar
on her lip. And because her lips continue
to move after she finishes speaking,
she reads the *Bible*, wears red flannel,
says she's the first female to speak
a silent tongue. The mystery
in her life centers on why she pours
ketchup across the periphery
of her burger before every bite,
why she refuses to eat scrambled eggs
unless she sprinkles a dash
of salt for each of pepper.
And because her left eye twitches
when she eats, she pitches her fork
into a piece of chocolate cream
pie and pops it in her mouth
for the cast of *Unsolved Mysteries,*
for the *National Enquirer,*
for *The Guinness Book of World Records.*

Governess-to-Go

Like a paramedic you're always prepared:
SunPass, GPS, several pairs of sunglasses stowed
in the glove compartment. The trunk, a mobile office
brimming with the stock of your trade: index cards,
grammar books, charged laptop. You enter their homes
like a priest, pet their little white dogs, blend into
their storyline. You worry about the gifted sixth-grader
who vomits the week before midterms. You tutor
the whiz kid who refuses to shave a barely-there mustache;
an aspiring video game designer with Asperger's,
he forgets to greet you at the door. You assist the Xbox
enthusiast who attempts great height with a voluminous
pompadour he teases into defying gravity. You help
the Brobdingnagian slacker inhabiting a universe ill-fitted
to skyscraping adolescence, an eighth-grader always
hunching to avoid bumping his head beneath doorways.
You try reaching the one who doesn't seem to care
about anything or anyone, drifts through days with earbuds
attached like he's plugged into the Matrix. You're up on the dirt:
the stingy ex-husband, the mother who forced her son to write
with his right even though he's a lefty, the girl who dozed
during SATs, the boy who seized in the crib and zips
his backpack shut after bullies spit inside, the moody
sophomore whose grades sky rocket when he starts dating—
whose *abuela* says he should first master keeping *calzoncillos*
clean. You cater to the protégé with the tiger mom who demands
you assign more homework. The kid never smiles
except when mentioning spies and favorite fictional character
Alex Rider. You tend to the secretive soccer player
who attempts texting during sessions, her fingertips sheathed
by band-aids. You worry about each one. You have no children
of your own. Logic says, *Don't get attached if they offer*

wallet-size senior pictures, friend you on Facebook,
or reveal tidbits the parents don't know. They'll move on.
They'll struggle to remember your name several years from now.
These kids, like fashions on the red carpet, are on loan.
After golden statuettes are distributed and after-parties fizzle,
sparkly pins and pavé rings return to the vault. Gauzy and
sequined gowns are zipped and taken to the mother ship.

Catching Edward

He's no Daddy Warbucks,
thinks Jane. Adèle's head
is often garnished with ash

from his havana. If he signs
adoption papers it won't stick.
His garbled calligraphy will

sprout wings and then it's back
to square one for the perfect
Parisian who pirouettes

for scraps of empty praise.
The women consider Adèle
a Frenchified fool, a firefly

somersaulting in midair.
Men in tails and top hats
speak in hushed tones,

muse at the charming
orphaned coquette
while unearthing cigars

from a box like cadavers.
They strain to observe
each gesture, each twist

of the small exquisite waist,
the circumference of dainty
wrists and fingers taking

flight. Jane feigns indifference,
thinks Adèle should cling
to minor comforts: Polaroids

of mama, evening prayers
to the Virgin, Pilot's tail wagging
in greeting. Being ignored

trumps staging an impromptu
ballet turned peep show
in hopes of getting a pat

on the back from Thornfield's
resident Baby Daddy,
in hopes of catching Edward.

Letter to Edward

*—I woke in the dark after dreaming I was buried alive,
and when I was awake the feeling of suffocation persisted.*
(from *Wide Sargasso Sea*, Jean Rhys)

Despite popular opinion, I don't hate you.
You're not evil. Just misguided. Too much of a yes man.
Marrying for big bucks not a brilliant career move.
Haters trash talk. Friends label you a glorified gigolo,
allege you turned Bertha into a Stepford wife,
then watched in dismay as the Caribbean queen
alternated between biting her toes and uprooting
clumps of hair when she believed the Gytrash's glowing
gaze penetrated her pores and scalp, when she swore
spirits sent secret messages—Morse code from the great
beyond disguised as a series of sneezes or twitches.
Communing with the dead came at a high price.
Medical bills multiplied. Doctors leeched her temples.
The quack who pushed the rest cure catapulted her
into a near catatonic state. You wish you didn't despise her.
The woman screws anything with a pulse and refuses to floss.
She snuck into your room and set your Tempur-Pedic on fire.
You're forever rubbing the spot where your wedding band
once resided. In dreams you lather your hand with butter,
but the ring refuses to budge, so you surrender the finger
to the saw's merciless blade. When your eyelids flutter
open at dawn the digit remains swollen, red, intact.
Despite the pathetic attempt at polygamy, I don't hate you.
You're no boy scout—but you're no Heathcliff either.
Cliff is capable of leaning over the roof and dangling
Big Bertha by the ankles just for kicks.
That SOB is likely to pop bubbly
as her skull cracks on cobblestone.

Marsh End Priestess

It was an ordinary morning.
I parked my red Corvette outside her studio
and drank a bottle of Pepsi from the Quick Seven.

I lowered the windows,
let the lawnmower's buzz, the radio's drone
massage me back to life after leaving the club,

the streets crowded with A-list party people
fleeing in sports cars, limos, taxis,
running from eleven kinds of loneliness,

from Godzillas, Mothras, and Ghidorahs,
all heads and arms and legs, mythological
creatures materializing, swooping

down to claw the contours of the human skull.
Still, I like to think I owned the night,
the part of it no one wants, the hours

between two and five, but night had dwindled,
chameleons were blending onto dry leaves
when I rang the doorbell and saw her rise from hiding

into sight like the moon, like a high priestess,
like light falling onto the sheets when you are sleeping.
I wanted a movie screen kiss,

asked if she'd elope. She laughed and let me in.
Her skin smelled like fresh bread.
She was smoking the butt of a cigarette,

its glowing red circle of ash grazing
her chipped fingernails. Her paintings conjured
visions of exotica, of electric blue and pink

seashells beneath a sky raining metal.
She showed me her latest work: man and woman
sitting on a white curtained bed. In the background,

a window through which a tree is seen,
a window through which everything begins
which has no meaning, only sound,

shrouded whispering in a wild tongue.

Jane Eyre: Classic Cover Girl

It looks like the beginning of the end.
Somber grays and charcoals match mournful

looks on Jane and Edward's faces. Atropos tightens
her grip on the thread of life with one hand,

around her infamous shears with the other.
Even Mesrour, Edward's steed, seems depressed.

Save us! Save us from ourselves! the three shout
telepathically. But wait! There's a fourth in this funeral

procession: *Pilot, the Peppy Pooch*. With perky ears
and grin, the playful pup photobombs this pic like a pro.

The Newfoundland radiates cheer as if belly and ears
are freshly rubbed. Puppy intuition warns Pilot

Thornfield will blow, so he basks in the afterglow
of eating Scooby Snacks like there's no tomorrow.

These girls look like there's no tomorrow.
Random House reminds readers why they despise

Lowood, brand it *Prep School Purgatory*.
Side-by-side in perfect rows these Christian clones

mirror the creepy kids in *Village of the Damned*.
Their shadows sad and nondescript, hair raked back,

shoulders stooped, eyes downcast, lids heavy as bricks.
I want to donate fur-lined boots, fleece scarves

and gloves. I want to bestow electric blankets
and heated toilet seats. Because each narrow waist

speaks of hunger, I want to herd the girls onto a bus
en route to Piccadilly Cafeteria or Cracker Barrel

for comfort food: cornbread, loaded potatoes,
hush puppies, mac-and-cheese.

꙳

A cheesy illustration graces French journal *Line*
in a bizarre attempt at a Nancy Drew cover.

The title should be *Jane Eyre Mystery Stories:*
The Clue in the Collapsing Castle. A winding dirt road

leads to Thornfield, a Transylvanian townhouse
with two spires piercing the evening sky like fangs.

One expects the terrible three—Lugosi, Karloff, Price—
and their ghoulish cronies will materialize from mist.

One assumes Hardy Boys (the Shaun Cassidy
and Parker Stevenson versions) will race to warn Jane,

who can probably pick up radio signals
with her Princess Leia updo, dispel fog

with her ludicrous Doris Day wardrobe,
a coral blouse and matching coral lipstick.

꙳

A stick is likely stowed in Rochester's garments
or a cane he'll use on Jane—Barnabas Collins

style or *Grand Theft Auto* style. *An Immortal Story
of Undying Love That's Pointed Straight at Your Heart*

boasts the Quick Reader edition. An Orson Welles-like
Rochester lurks in the rear, fur-collared riding cloak

draped across his shoulders clasped with a gold chain
he considers using mafia style in lieu of piano

wire for strangling the governess whose colossal head
cocked to the right prompts Brits to christen the pic

Jane Eyre: Bauble Head. Eyre's Joan Fontaine-inspired
eyebrows are penciled to perfection. Her look-at-me

lashes and aloof pouty lips seem to say,
Read me. Read me now.

⬭

*Read me. Read me now, The Tempestuous Temptress
of Thornfield,* a Harlequin-inspired spoof beckons.

She'll be sorry for canoodling with the missionary,
thinks Rochester, who's exceeded his cursing quota

and looks like Wolverine. The big brute contorts
his mouth about to snarl or spit a wad of tobacco

at Jane's nape. He's repulsed yet drawn to Jane,
a Liz Taylor impersonator, who tries to pass

off a black nightie as an empire-waist gown.
Dark tresses cascade wantonly about her shoulders

and back as she embodies the starlet
and gazes into the distance, lips parted,

about to discover the meaning of life
or perhaps a better prospect.

∾

Prospective readers face an angry Edward
who's got his dukes up in what Brontëites

have dubbed *The Boxing Buffoon.*
Is he giving the Gothic heroine fighting tips?

Perhaps it's a self-protective gesture,
the pretty boy trying to preserve a glass jaw

for a spread in *Big and Bigamous.*
Maybe he's undercover for the *Fashion Police,*

about to deflate Jane's puffy sleeves with a right
and left cross. The sleeves look like footballs

or floaties foreshadowing she's going to jump
ship before a boudoir brawl begins

and her frou-frou dress gets ripped
by Team Rochester or by Big Bad Bertha.

∾

Big Bad Bertha is drawn as a candle-holding
crypt keeper in Everyman's Library pencil sketch,
a compelling endorsement for *Why Women Should Wear
Wrinkle Cream.* Her face a maze of deep-set lines.
A cover designed before zombie fever re-infected

pop culture, before *The Walking Dead*,
Zombie Undead, or even *Shaun of the Dead*.
Bertha resembles one of the females
in *The Return of the Living Dead*,
or rather, the severed and rotting head
strapped to a gurney in the mortuary.
Reanimated by noxious gas, the zombie explains
how the pain of being dead is assuaged
by an all-you-can-eat buffet of *brains, brains, brains*.

Brainy Jane protects her noggin
in a Signet Classic worthy of the name
Jane and the Cutthroat Cape. A huge collar
Vader or Voldemort would favor
obstructs her peripheral vision. Retractable
knives eject from the sides when someone stands
too close on the Tube, a feature attractive enough
to entice slice-and-dice boys Jason, Freddy, Michael—
which leads us to believe Jane stows cutlery
in her collar to shield her best asset,
the seat of her intelligence, because of Bertha's
venomous bite, because Mason is a night crawler
now, an undead degenerate trolling for victims
in hopes of satiating an infinite hunger.

An infinite hunger will plague Mason,
who looks like he's been mauled
by a panther or a blood-sucking *chupacabra*.
The party crasher and his sister will be labeled
Satan's Spawn: Zombie Siblings From Hell.
I've lost Bertha forever, he thinks.
She doesn't even recognize her own brother.

Mason is propped on pillows as Jane tends the bite.
Soon bleeding will cease. Rigor mortis will set in.
Unable to locate a heartbeat or pulse,
Dr. Carter will be miffed. But you and I,
Reader, we'll recognize the telltale signs:
vitals on strike, atypical pallor, a brief respite
from pain. It's the beginning of the end.

Promiscuous Reading

Reading *Jane Eyre* II

I opened a can of alphabet soup
and searched for clues in letters,
life preservers in broth.
I watched the evening news expecting
her body in a lake, her bleached
hair smeared across the water's surface
smooth as straw. I fingered the kitchen
counter, decrypted each cookie crumb.
I checked the billiard table pockets,
behind the bathroom mirror,
between the lampshade's pleats.
Later, I dreamt my left foot was bootless,
bruised by gravel when I read her
signature in the quiet grace of a passing cloud.

Reading *Jane Slayre*

—*Reader, I buried him.*
   (from *Jane Slayre*, Sherri Erwin)

After reading *Jane Eyre*, I fell in love with Jane Slayre,
the tiny female Van Helsing-like avenger who eradicates

unruly members of the undead—a vocation confirmed when
John Reed tries to gobble the destitute orphan like a Little Debbie

Snack Cake. I admire Jane's ingenuity and foresight,
hours employed gathering and sharpening wood, stakes always

up her sleeve or stowed beneath her skirt in case VSP
(vampiric sensory perception) kicks in. I admire the quick draw.

Nimble fingers unsheathing Egyptian daggers,
a beloved keepsake from Ms.Temple for severing zombie

heads despite the inevitable aftermath of green goo
that will coat Jane's pinafore and stockings like nuclear waste.

Reader, I found myself rooting for a literary smackdown
between the bloodsucking Blanche and the jaguarish Jane.

I wanted what countless women have wanted: to cheer
and do the wave as Jane drives a stake through her rival's

shriveled heart. Miss Ingram, the unrepentant socialite guilty
of precipitating her own demise, of prematurely turning into a pile

of dust at Jane's feet, the penalty exacted for chomping
on little Adèle's thighs like a pair of KFC drumsticks.

Jane Responds When Asked, *Why Edward?*

It's spring in the park.
We stroll in silence.

Edward's cigar cocked
to the side. Both hands intact.

The pupil and iris in each eye healthy.
The scar anointing furrowed

forehead, severing an eyebrow
in two, is absent. Ahead,

an older couple stranded
in a red surrey try pedaling up

an incline and beyond the asphalt's
grassy treachery. Who knows how long

they've been huffing and puffing
pitiably like upside-down turtles.

Edward approaches from behind
and gives a gentle push propelling

the surrey into the afternoon light.
A guardian spirit, he remains unseen,

content blowing smoky haloes,
observing dragonfly flight patterns,

the unlikely elegance of hindwings
broader than forewings on a mating pair

of marsh skimmers perched on a twig.

Postmortem Lament for Charlotte

—Arthur says such letters as mine never ought to be kept—they are
dangerous as Lucifer matches.
(Charlotte Brontë to Ellen Nussey; letter dated 1854)

You're a commodity now. They will pillage your life.
They will raid the closets of your memory—
auctioning, trading, and stealing your correspondence
for posterity, entertainment, or several hundred pounds.
Everyone will know you had the hots for your French
teacher because his wife will salvage your ripped
scrawl from the trash and stitch the pieces together with cotton
and gum. Everyone will get the dish on daddy's drinking problem,
will discover your little brother bagged an older babe,
a married woman named (appropriately enough) Mrs. Robinson.
Collectors will covet the grayish, black-bordered mourning
paper you used after Branwell and Emily are interred
in the parsonage graveyard, Anne in Scarborough,
will hunt the five fragments scattered across Haworth,
Dublin, Texas, New York, and Pennsylvania. Your life smudged
by a combination of familiar and foreign fingerprints,
riddled with scratches and Ellen's deletions.
Cutouts. Your dad will become the favored pen pal of enthusiasts.
His well-intentioned mutilations resulting in relics—
strips of cursive distributed like lotto tickets
to faithful Brontëites fascinated by your small scribble,
its looped-back *d*s and sharply-angled *y* tails
now faded to a light brown.

The Literature of Prescription

—Live as domestic a life as possible . . . and never touch pen, brush or pencil as long as you live. (Charlotte Perkins Gilman describes Dr. S. Weir Mitchell's advice, 1913)

This is what the doctor prescribed.
Perhaps she trusted him because of the paternal
eyes, well-groomed beard and commanding stethoscope.
Praised by Freud, females flocked to Mitchell's
sanitarium. He was a renowned rest cure expert.
She a thwarted activist, an ambivalent wife and despondent
mother. Perhaps Perkins thought she needed to relent.
Surrendering the juggling act and handing
over the reins initially comforting.
Next month, tomorrow, right now irrelevant.
Acquiescence her new best friend, a silent partner,
an ally persuading her to abandon plans for saving
the world, coaxing her to ignore the calendar,
ditch the wrist watch, draw the curtains.

Keeping blackout curtains drawn
and lingering in bed a little longer
a temptation one always faces during days
of endless rain in the Sunshine State
where neighboring streets threaten flood,
humidity swallows all rational thought,
and the barometric pressure, flighty tramp,
forces the right side of my head to throb like an expectant
cock. Stormy days I yearn for the clichéd return to womb,
desire to exchange one form of solitude for another,
to swap an imperfect quiet for a restful silence.
Instead, I insert earplugs to muffle the impertinent
downpour and settle for the bedroom's embryonic darkness
while my husband inhabits the library's calm pallor.

A medical librarian, my husband researches
new treatments hoping to discover a therapy

that will extract the ache from my head
the way tweezers remove a splinter.

Versed in the language of pain, the vernacular
of Chronic Daily Headache (CDH) infiltrates

the mundane: sumatriptans, ergotamines, NSAIDS,
MAOIS, serotonin syndrome, rebound headache.

Mornings my husband prepares a vitamin cocktail
of milk thistle, fish oil, feverfew, B6, B100, and butterbur.

He deposits the capsules inside a pillbox labeled *breakfast,
lunch, afternoon, bedtime*. Before grabbing briefcase

and coffee cup and vanishing into the congested city,
he places the pillbox on the kitchen counter like a valentine.

An unlikely valentine, I down the pills
to ward off the frequency and severity of CDH,
classified as experiencing 15 or more days
per month with headache. A rare breed, CDH patients
are wired with a hyper-excitable cerebral cortex,
with abnormal control of pain neurons in the brainstem.
The body is duped into believing pain normal.
Cells are held hostage by the choreography of an infinite loop,
the headache cycle akin to a needle stuck in a record's groove.

At onset pain is a malevolent presence searing the scalp
every second, a hot poker pinching the neck,
forceps continually clamping the temples.
Chronic headaches torment an unfortunate 4 to 5 percent
who are unresponsive to most meds.

I'm unresponsive to Topomax, Percocet, Frova.
I have a greater chance of getting buzzed
off the scent of shampoo than from Oxycontin.
Because of our bodies' stubborn indifference to meds,
many female patients are written off as psychosomatic
or hysterical. My own Weir Mitchell, my first neurologist
proposed a creative remedy for my malaise.
Head cocked, seated on his big leathery chaise,
the physician gave me the once-over, then soberly
proclaimed I *needed* a boyfriend. Maybe he envisioned
my vagina dilapidated and at the mercy of cobwebs.
        Did anyone offer similar counsel to C.B.?
Her letters mention facial neuralgia, disenchanted days
bedridden, head throbbing, wind howling across desolate moors.

Brontë's head throbbed as wind howled across desolate moors.
She suffered acutely when winter gales buffeted Haworth.

Primitive migraine remedies included ingesting
arsenic, citric acid, brain duster tablets,

and Wolcott's Instant Pain Annihilator
(two of its known ingredients opium and ethyl alcohol).

Ads for Wolcott's syrup depict a man besieged
by demons: the headache demon sits on the forehead,

one leg perched on each brow, a pair of neuralgic
demons jab at teeth with pickax and pitchfork.

At times Brontë pushed past this discomfort,
channeled lambasting pain into pristine prose.

Perhaps she would've been more prolific without
migraine—without Robert Southey's infamous advice.

⌒

The poet laureate's infamous advice reminiscent of Dr. Mitchell's:

The daydreams in which you habitually indulge
are likely to induce a distempered state of mind,
& in proportion as "all the ordinary uses of the world"
seem to you "flat & unprofitable," you will be unfitted
for them, without becoming fitted for anything else.

Literature cannot be the business of a woman's life,
& it ought not to be. The more she is engaged
in her proper duties, the less leisure will she have for it . . . .

Charlotte Perkins Gilman renounced the rest cure,
recovered and wrote *The Yellow Wallpaper*.
Charlotte Brontë followed Southey's admonition selectively,
writing as a means of *soothing the mind & elevating it—*
which is also what the poet prescribed.

St. John Rivers Pops the Question

*—I have lately met with a wonder, a man who thinks Jane Eyre would have
done better [to] marry Mr. Rivers!* (Mary Taylor to Charlotte Brontë; letter
dated June / July 24, 1848)

You've waited for a proposal since playing house
and roaming Aunt Reed's herb garden in your nightgown,
wearing a white pillowcase for a veil as you plucked
sweet peas, a collar of eucalyptus leaves, a sprig
of bleeding hearts from the earth's damp mouth.
The man who lusts after your mind—*only*—who finagled
you into giving up German to learn Hindustani
so the two of you can get hitched, jet to India, and save the world
stands before you stiff as a ceramic groom for the top tier
of your wedding cake. The cassock drapes across his legs
like a bell-shaped flower. You're tempted to bury your face
in the quiet of each fold, each delicate crease unfurling
at the sound of your voice, at the slightest graze of a curious
fingertip. Unlike Eddie, he doesn't expect you to register
for Whitecliff or Wedgewood ASAP, for the cobalt crystal
water jug, goblets and sherry glasses, the matching champagne
flutes. He doesn't demand you tie the knot in a Princess Di
ensemble, the ivory silk-crepe gown and jacket auctioned
at Christie's, or a satin floral brocade with a scoop neck
and cathedral-length skirt. However, you can't even blink
or move, like when Bertha snuck into your room and lurked over
your four-post bed and you thought she'd slit your throat
with her glittery ghetto nails. Instead, the klepto lifted
your Vera Wang veil, a gift from Eddie. You were afraid
of winding up like her brother, Mason, chest unzipped,
on the bare mattress like a yellow-tailed snapper waiting
to be gutted. You feared sleep, nightmares—bloody sponges
floating in basins, Bertha opening her mouth to flash
a sharp fang until you awoke burdened, limbs to the mattress
like a circus elephant manacled to the ground.
If it were up to Miss Loony Tunes she'd rip that row

of shiny buttons right off JR's cassock, sink her claws
into his tender torso like barbs of stinging nettle,
hooked bristles along the edge of cutgrass,
he'd learn the difference between *yes* and *no*,
between *I do* and *I don't*.

Jane Eyre: Heiress, Avon Lady, Plastic Surgery Junkie

> *. . . if God had gifted me with some beauty and much wealth . . . .*
> (from *Jane Eyre,* Charlotte Brontë)

Your uncle kicks the bucket and suddenly you're rich.
No more checking the Sunday paper for coupons,
no more five-dollar-all-you-can-eat China Buffet,
scouring dollar stores for cheap Christmas gifts:
scented candles, *salsero* Santas, and plastic nativity sets
where baby Jesus looks like a ghost. After you donate
your ten percent to the church you can charge the hundred-dollar
ionic blow dryer, the massage chair, and the heat-activated
pillow from Sharper Image. You can get collagen injections
for those meager lips, some Botox to counteract lines
around the edges of your mouth, and you can liven up the girls—
Eddie calls them Thelma and Louise—with a much needed lift.
Still, after this you'll look in the mirror each morning
and worry Eddie thinks Blanche is more beautiful,
and when you die mourners will hold hands
like mass-produced paper dolls.
Cloistered inside your coffin like a pearl,
like a life-size chess piece wrapped in white linen,
a few relics will sustain you in the next life:
make-up kit, emerald-encrusted mirror, gilt comb with shark
teeth tines. Demoted on the evolutionary ladder you'll reincarnate
as an Avon Lady or one of those Mary Kay creme puffs
cruising in a pink Cadillac, peddling cosmetics to reluctant
housewives half your age, and the women, girls really, will stare
beyond your Sally Jessy glasses, mesmerized by crow's feet
you've tried to camouflage with jars of vanishing cream.
You'll dye your pubes royal plum.
You'll brag you've walked the runways in Milan,
been coronated Thistle Queen of Scotland, dabbled
with Don Juans promising diamonds big as Texas.

You'll wave your hands for emphasis, big globs of fake gold
orbiting your fingers as you point to Avon catalogue page five
and say, *Every fashionista knows three is a charm,*
that's why this genuine three-stone cubic zirconium pendant
represents your past, present, and future.

Jane Dreams of Rescuing Helen

She hacked bloody mucous, made two fists,
then pummeled her chest trying to breathe.

I woke to her lifeless form,
one hand splayed against the bedrail,

the other still gripping an inhaler. I've traced
the inscription on her tombstone with my forefinger.

When AMBER Alerts flash, I suspect
Brocklehurst and Scatcherd faked her death,

then auctioned her to a child prostitution ring
in Guatemala or perhaps as a mail-order bride in Thailand

where she's bewildered by the language and landscape,
by swarms of balding men, each old enough to be her father.

In my daydreams, she kneels and prays God will appoint me
the agent of her deliverance. After rescuing Helen we return

to Northumberland where she wanders across familiar
moorland, observes curlicues soaring overhead,

bills curled downward in greeting. Helen is eventually adopted
by wealthy New Zealanders, doting parents who say her beauty

surpasses Helen of Troy's as they tuck her in bed.
Her favorite pets, Francis and Clare, a pair of sheep

she takes to show-and-tell and parades at local fairs.
She displays their award ribbons and medals beside the gold-

enameled teapot in her mother's china cabinet.
On Halloween she dresses as Little Bo-Peep and takes

Francis and Clare trick-or-treating, makes rounds at nativity plays,
the placid sheep always reposing beside baby Jesus's manger.

As an adult, Helen transitions from beloved Sunday school teacher
to well-known televangelist, millions tuning in to hear the Word

as they sip morning coffee. The image of Helen's kind face
and relaxed demeanor while reading scripture remains with them,

changes their lives in subtle ways. Audience members refrain
from nail biting, cutting in traffic or at checkout,

from spanking children for minor offenses. A staunch viewer,
St. John admires Helen's dynamic preaching and missionary work.

He shreds Rosamond's picture. After a brief introduction
and whirlwind romance, St. John and Helen exchange vows

and head to India where camera crews film their experiences
as part of a new Christian reality show. Always a brainiac,

Helen's aptitude for languages enables her to pick up Hindustani
faster than I ever could. A byproduct of Scatcherd's punishments,

she's developed a high threshold for tolerating discomfort
and never complains of sweltering heat. Her indomitable spirit

always inspires St. John's fervent admiration.
A devoted husband, he thanks his Maker for Helen's piety

and patience—for the beautiful blaze of hair
he unpins and brushes after evening prayer.

Jane Eyre Thinks of Tarzan's Jane at Canton's

—His stay in the West Indies has changed him out of all
knowledge. He has grey in his hair and misery in his eyes.
(from *Wide Sargasso Sea,* Jean Rhys)

We eat here because it is quick, cheap, and delicious.
Underneath the table your fingers touch the almost nakedness

of my sandaled feet. Fried noodles in a bamboo bowl
resemble chopped vines, remind me of Sunday afternoons

squandered watching old Tarzan flicks while munching
on noodles from takeout. Johnny Weissmuller swung

fearlessly from vines, bare feet dangling in mid-flight,
then traipsing through dirt and mud. Johnny once chased

women on the studio lot sans loincloth.
I think of loincloths and love in the tree house,

of Tarzan caressing the soles of Jane's feet
the way you caress mine, of Jane wrapping the vines

of her legs around the apeman's waist in the jungle night
as he buries his face in her curly hair, strong as vines

and dark as night, as mine, which you tug
and often envision billowing underwater,

though I know you're not immersed in the jungle
recreating scenes from *Tarzan and His Mate.*

The jungle, *that green menace,* too much like Jamaica:
dusty, reminiscent of sunburns, of feverish nights

spent swatting mosquitoes that boldly alighted
on your neck. No tree house for you. Nix the vines.

Ditto on the refined Maureen O'Sullivan.
I've usually lost you to a concrete jungle,

to *Splash* and Daryl Hannah when you part my
drenched hair and fan each half over a neighboring breast.

Letter to Bertha

—There are always two deaths, the real one and the one people know about.
(from *Wide Sargasso Sea*, Jean Rhys)

If I could, I'd save you.
Flies beneath your bed hiss *Bertha, Antoinette,*
Bertha—though you plug your ears
with lima beans, syllables seep
in like dust pushing past closed shutters,
like locoweed creeping across the garden wall,
the mute battlements. Better to bust out of your cell,
to let the oversized roach motel burn
before your so-called-husband stuffs you
in a body bag, seals you like a cracker in a Ziploc.
I'd set you up in a beachside condo
stocked with your favorite dahlias:
Arabian Nights, Black Satins, Burma Gems.
I'd hire a good massage therapist and enroll
you in yoga. I'd take you to a spa,
treat you to a mud bath, restore those charcoal
stained feet to their original hue,
have a stylist trim that cavewoman hair.
You'd take up kickboxing and swimming.
You'd see a shrink who specializes in pyromania,
who'd prescribe an antidepressant cocktail
for those unpredictable mood swings and panic attacks.
After shopping for a new wardrobe, a red dress
and matching sling-backs, we'd climb the Statue of Liberty,
we'd toss your straight jacket into the ocean,
and along with it each vestige of sadness
that has tinged your bloodshot eyes.
I'd make you forget Edward.
I'd cradle your face in my hands and I'd kiss you,
a hypnotic lip-lock extinguishing each bad memory,
obliterating suffering from your lexicon.
Bertha, if I could, I'd save you.

The Appropriation of Jane

Juana was the conquistadors' name for Cuba.
Juana is the Spanish equivalent of Jane.

Juana is thick as *queso crema*
slathered across the tongue.

Juana rhymes with iguana.
Juana pushes past the slit of our lips.

Juana is the sound that escapes
before we regurgitate.

Juana was a worker ant in a past life.
Juana fed the Queen by cramming

food retched from her stomach
into her Majesty's cavernous mouth.

Spain's Majesty, the Queen of Castile
played harpsichord, monochord, guitar

before confinement in a convent,
before society branded her *Juana la Loca.*

Others gossiped about a different Juana,
Mexico's Tenth Muse, self-taught scholar

and poet of the Baroque School,
Sor Juana Inés de la Cruz.

So many interesting Juanas—
but enough—I'm ditching Juana.

This poem is not about Juana.
This poem is about Jane: Mary Jane,

Lady Jane, Crazy Jane, Baby Jane.
In Hebrew Jane means graced by Yahweh.

This poem is about Saint Jane Frances de Chantal
whose soul ascended like a celestial fireball,

busty Janes and platinum blonde Janes:
Russell, Fonda, Mansfield,

cross-dressing and cigar-smoking Janes
like Addams and Calamity.

This poem is about the quintessential
Plain Jane: Jane Eyre, who graciously helps

birth poems stubborn as kidney stones,
mischievous poems that hopscotch

across the page because I've ripped
off Charlotte Brontë's heroine,

pinned the Gothic girl against my bulletin board
like tabloid trivia, a wisp of licorice,

Jane who is pristine, precise, polished,
Jane who is simple, sweet, succinct.

At the British Library

Charlotte's manuscript sepulchered
like an incorruptible saint,

splayed on its back like a woman
whose architecture I want to touch,

to trace the arc of her earlobes,
taste her delicate torso, swallow

the goodness spilling from both breasts,
from the crevice between her legs,

ingest her jutting shoulder blades,
drench myself with her rhapsodic scent,

trap her longhand beneath
the drawbridge of my tongue.

Notes

The poem "Cross-Dressing" was inspired by the first chapter of Sandra M. Gilbert and Susan Gubar's classic feminist text *The Madwoman in the Attic: The Woman Writer and the Nineteenth-Century Literary Imagination* (1979). Gilbert and Gubar explore the notion and metaphor of literary paternity. *Is a pen a metaphorical penis?* they ask. *Where does such [a] . . . patriarchal theory of literature leave literary women? If the pen is a metaphorical penis, with what organs can females generate texts?*

References to Charlotte Brontë's correspondence are based on *The Letters of Charlotte Brontë: With a Selection of Letters by Family and Friends*. Volume I: 1829-1847 (1995). Volume II: 1848-1851 (2000). Volume III: 1852-1855 (2004). Each volume is edited by Margaret Smith.

The following phrases appear in Charlotte Brontë's novel *Jane Eyre* (1847):

Bewick's *History of British Birds* is mentioned in chapter 1.

. . . shores of Lapland, Siberia, Spitzbergen, Nova Zembla, Iceland . . . are mentioned in chapter 1.

. . . a bird rending its own plumage . . . is spoken by Edward Rochester in chapter 23.

Treacherous slate is mentioned in chapter 7.

Tenacious of life is spoken by Edward Rochester in chapter 13.

The phrase "That green menace" originally appears in Jean Rhys's postcolonial novel *Wide Sargasso Sea* (1966), considered a prequel to *Jane Eyre*.

Under the principle of "fem[m]e covert," a woman, upon her marriage, became one with her husband in the eyes of the law. She becomes a covered [or hidden] woman . . . (from Debra Teachman's *Understanding Jane Eyre: A Student Casebook to Issues, Sources, and Historical Documents*, 2001).

"Alice Fairfax in Wonderland" was inspired by Franco Mondini-Ruiz's 2009 mixed media installation, *Crystal City*—which is part of *Our America: The Latino Presence in American Art*, an exhibition drawn from the Smithsonian American Art Museum's collection of Latino art. In *Crystal City*, items like silverware and stemware are arranged in a grid pattern on a low pedestal. The installation is titled after a small town that was the birthplace of the Chicano civil rights movement in Texas.

Some of the covers described in "Jane Eyre: Classic Cover Girl" are actual book covers; others are spoofs created by fans. Most of the images are available on Google by using the search phrases "Jane Eyre covers" and "Jane Eyre images."

Principes Negros means dark princes and are roses of a deep red hue.

The poem title "The Literature of Prescription" is borrowed from the title of an exhibit provided by The History of Medicine Division of the National Library of Medicine. *The Literature of Prescription: Charlotte Perkins Gilman and "The Yellow Wall-Paper"* examines a nineteenth-century writer's challenge to the medical profession and the relationship between science and society. The exhibit consists of six free-standing graphic panels.

The section title "Promiscuous Reading" is a phrase that appears in Joyce Carol Oates's *Jane Eyre: An Introduction*. "[The Brontë children] . . . were influenced by their father's storytelling and by their wide and promiscuous reading . . . ."

Statistics on CDH appear in Paula Kamen's 2005 memoir *All in My Head: An Epic Quest to Cure an Unrelenting, Totally Unreasonable, and Only Slightly Enlightening Headache* (Da Capo Press). Chapter one states, "Yet, as more recent studies have shown, CDH actually affects only 4-5 percent of the population . . . ." Chapter 21 specifies that ". . . drugs available for CDH prevention only really work in about 50 percent of patients (and even they should expect, at most, a 50 percent reduction in pain)."

I compiled lines for the cento "Marsh End Priestess" as an assignment for *Special Topics: Trends in Contemporary Poetry— Literary Collaboration and Collage*, a graduate seminar taught by Denise Duhamel at Florida International University in 2001. Mitch Alderman, Terri Carrion, Andreé Conrad, Kendra Dwelley Guimaraes, Wayne Loshusan, Abigail Martin, Estee Mazor, Astrid Parrish, Stacy Richardson, Sandy Rodriguez, Jay Snodgrass, Richard Toumey, George Tucker, Jennifer Welch, William Whitehurst, and I contributed individual lines.

Glossary

Sherri Browning Erwin is the author of *Jane Slayre* (2010), a horror, mash-up novel based on *Jane Eyre.*

Charlotte Perkins Gilman (1860–1935) was an American sociologist; novelist; writer of short stories, poetry, and nonfiction; and a lecturer for social reform. She wrote her semi-autobiographical short story, *The Yellow Wallpaper,* after a severe bout of postpartum depression.

Constantin Georges Romain Héger (1809–1896) was a Belgian teacher and, for a time, the object of Charlotte Brontë's unrequited infatuation. He instructed Charlotte and Emily Brontë during the 1840s in Brussels.

Henry Maudsley (1835–1918) was a British psychiatrist. His textbooks include *The Physiology and Pathology of Mind* (1867) and *Mental Responsibility in Health and Disease* (1874).

Arthur Bell Nicholls (1819–1906) was Charlotte Brontë's husband and spent his life as curator of her memory.

Ellen Nussey (1817–1897) was a lifelong friend and correspondent of Charlotte Brontë. More than 500 letters received from Nussey influenced Elizabeth Gaskell's 1857 biography *The Life of Charlotte Brontë.*

Laci Denise Peterson (1975–2002) was an American woman who went missing while seven-and-a-half months pregnant with her first child. Her husband, Scott Peterson, was later convicted of murder in the first degree for Laci and in the second degree for their prenatal son, Conner.

Robert Southey (1774–1843) was an English poet of the Romantic school, one of the Lake Poets, and Poet Laureate of England for 30 years.

About the Author

Rita Maria Martinez is a Writing Consultant for Nova Southeastern University, where she teaches composition workshops for nursing students and tutors undergraduate and graduate students. Martinez is also an independent reading and writing tutor. Her poetry appears in various literary journals and magazines, including *Gulf Stream Magazine* and *Tigertail: A South Florida Poetry Annual*. Her work also appears in the eighth edition of Stephen Minot's textbook *Three Genres: The Writing of Fiction/Literary Nonfiction, Poetry and Drama* (Prentice Hall); and in the anthology *Burnt Sugar, Caña Quemada: Contemporary Cuban Poetry in English and Spanish* (Simon & Schuster). Martinez has been a featured author at the Miami Book Fair International; at the Society of the Four Arts in Palm Beach, Florida; and at the *Palabra Pura* reading series sponsored by the Guild Literary Complex in Chicago. She earned an MFA in Creative Writing from Florida International University. Visit Martinez's website at www.comeonhome.org/ritamartinez.

Made in the USA
Middletown, DE
19 August 2018